Stealthy Darkness

Gene Toews

Copyright © 2020 by Gene Toews.

ISBN-978-1-6455-0826-7

All rights reserved. No part of this book may be reproduced or transmitted in any form or by any means, electronic or mechanical, including photocopying, recording, or by any information storage and retrieval system, without permission in writing from the copyright owner.

The views expressed in this work are solely those of the author and do not necessarily reflect the views of the publisher, and the publisher hereby disclaims any responsibility for them.

Matchstick Literary
1-888-306-8885
orders@matchliterary.com

Contents

Mama's and Daddy's Journey 1
The Storm 2
Rag Doll 3
Hacksaw Thunder 5
Going Home 7
Read on My Friend 9
I Am Stung 10
My Confession 11
On The Breeze 13
Writhing Elegance 14
Nature's Beast 15
My Shadow Fades 16
A Way Of Life 17
Relentless 19
Dragon's Kiss 21
Touch The Sun 22
I Am Life 23
In The Morning 26
Angels and Demons 28
Don't Look Back 31
I Am Fire 32
A Crippling Display 34
No Longer Missed 36
Wrath of the Gods 38
Raven's Roost 40
I Must Be Blessed 42
In The Valley 43
Sly Sunlight 44
Are You A Messiah 48

The Hurricane 51
Time To Rise 52
Chaos Is Perfection 54
Shh 56
Cries of War 58
The Charming Serpent 59
Smiles Or Tears 61
Saint Vincent 62
Odin's Birds 64
Fallen Angel 66
Nothing Personal 68
Deadly Beaks 69
The Darkness 70
Haunted 72
Plummeting 74
Entranced 75

Mama's and Daddy's Journey

My daddy was a blasphemer
He spoke to Lord's name in vain
My mama was a Christian woman
Even God couldn't keep her sane

My daddy, he ran with the devil
He was truly bad to the bone
My mama lived in an asylum
It was built out of brick and stone

My daddy's on the highway to hell
He's sowing seeds of evil
My mama doesn't believe he's bad
She prays for his soul's retrieval

My daddy made a jailbreak
It didn't work out so well
My mama dreamt of butterflies
It's all she had, in her padded cell

My daddy died with guns blazing
A symphony of destruction
My mama died of a broken heart
It was pulmonary obstruction

My daddy, he has earned his wings
He is an angel of hell
My mama is now totally sane
She is up where the Angels dwell

The Storm

The storm rips through the silence
Breathe deep in the driving rain
The fierce downpour has washed me clean
No more anguish. No more pain

The storm is raging in the night
I'm so beat down, I am crawling
The clouds open up. My head's pounding
Thunder erupts. The sky is falling

I have no fear of the storm
I'll meet it's fury in the night
God of Thunder says rest in peace
God of Lightning takes your sight

The savage storm has blurred my vision
Obscured the line between right and wrong
My will to survive remains unchanged
The Devil's choir sings a lovely song

The storm is finally over
There's a thick mist in the trees
The mist is burned off by the sun
The rest is whisked away by the breeze

Ride the storm into oblivion
Is there refuge in the eye?
The storm will carry me away
Into eternity. Goodbye

Rag Doll

The wolf's kingdom is the world
He's the king of all he surveys
His only enemy is man
Roaming free till the end of his days

The wolf's howl is bone chilling
Perhaps he's howling at the moon
Tell me. Is he calling your name
Control your fear on this night of doom

The wolf's eyes glow in the darkness
Totally still in the dusk
Your scent is on the breeze
He can smell your fear over his musk

The wolf's dreams are of carnage
Kill or be killed in the night
The wolf will not apologize
It does not kill for spite

The wolf's mercy does not exist
He is the perfect carnivore
Living and dying by the kill
The wolf sees food. You see gore

The wolf's sense of smell is keen
It smells you and knows your meat
You're between a rock and a hard place
You don't have the option to retreat

The wolf's instinct is natural
But he's just a beast of bone and hair
He kills. But he kills to eat
Mesmerized by his haunting stare

The wolf's hunger is legendary
He has a voracious appetite
Always searching. Always stalking
To hunt and kill his his birthright

The wolf's claws sink deep in your skin
With all your strength, you fight to survive
Pray all you want. Hell awaits
Primal instincts are keeping you alive

The wolf's teeth are long and sharp
They are designed to rend and tear
He is always in search of meat
The wolf is hunting. Beware

The wolf's prowling across the land
Patiently tracking his prey
Hot winds of death are blowing
You're not meant to live another day

The wolf's touch is not gentle
He will not caress you with teeth or claws
He will fight you to the death
Until you rag doll in his jaws

The End

Hacksaw Thunder

Reach out and touch the light
Would you utter your final prayer?
Lightning is the power of life
There's electricity is in the air

Still hopeful in the gloom?
Can you watch the sunrise?
Lightning blinds. Can't you see?
Can't see the beauty before your eyes

Unpredictable and deadly
Shocking power from the sky
Lightning. Fills the air like fire
Prayed for peace. Got no reply

My frail faith has deserted me
First searching for. Now reaching for the light
Lightning burns. There is no doubt
The blinding flash will excite

Like the hum of a million bees
Can you hear that buzzing sound
Lightning flashes. My fight for life
Raging thunder all around

Lightning and thunder in the storm
From night to day in an instant
Lightning zigzags to my feet
The thunder's rumble is not distant

Mother nature is humbling
Tearing its way through the night
Lightning is unpredictable
Pure power in a bolt of light

All will try. Most will fail
The strong and lucky might survive
Lightning splits the sky in two
Man and beast run for their lives

The hand of God strikes in the forest
Instantly the trees Ignite
Lightning. The harbinger of doom
Chase away the dark of night

In the power and rage of the storm
The battle starts to save my soul
Lightning descends. The nightmare begins
You can't claim to be in control

I am in the eye of the storm
Wicked thunderbolt rips the air
Lightning is slashing destruction
Smoking clothes and singed hair

Don't be fooled by it's beauty
Hacksaw thunder will steal your breath
Lightning burns. Run for your life
Ride the storm. Ride with death

The End

Going Home

This raven sings rock of ages
Ruthless and proud. It's my time
I welcome the night with my song
My croaking voice is sublime

This raven's mind is twisted
Can you feel my immortality?
Behold the beautiful carnage
This is my raving mentality

This raven will not be captured
I'm half obscured by the night
My croaking cry is ominous
I am the ravenous appetite

This raven rides on the wind
This bird of the night circles it's prey
This raven understands patience
You're to be scavenged. You may pray

This raven will not ask forgiveness
Repent for what? Am I to blame?
I'll not fall into that trap
I'll not live a life of shame

This raven has seen better days
My wing is broken. I can't fly.
I stare longingly at the wind
I want to soar up in the sky

This raven is not alone
Unkindness of ravens, darkens the sky
Search for death. Search for meat
Our ceaseless hunger you can't deny

This raven is not good or evil
I am only a hungry bird
Left to scavenge upon the world
Malicious intent. Absurd

This raven must whisper farewell
I'm beaten. I'm all out of fight
I say goodbye to the earth
My time is done. I whisper good night

This raven is going to the darkside
I am never to be seen again
This raven is going home
Forever and ever amen

The End

Read on My Friend

Dancing in the silence of the dawn
When day and night blend
Would you listen to fools for wise words?
Then by all means. Read on my friend

Dancing to the rhythm of hope
All of my cares are fading away
Black shadows run and hide
Before the light of a new day

Dancing to set my soul free
Have you ever had sex in the rain?
Lightning crashing all around you
Feels so good. You feel no pain

Dancing in the light of the stars
My mind is clear. My eyes are ablaze
There are no words for what I see
Into infinity I gaze

Dancing in the heat of desire
It's hot as the eye of the sun
Call of the wild is loud and clear
The forbidden dance has begun

Dancing on my shallow grave
Covered by dirt but my spirit is free
I'm no longer shackled to earth
Do not shed your tears for me

I Am Stung

The pursuit of truth is endless
The wind is blowing through the trees
Saint or sinner? I don't care
We are nothing but smoke in the breeze

I am on the edge of tomorrow
I am frail but I am strong
Win or lose? I don't care
I am right but I'm still wrong

I'm confused by your rhetoric
Eternal life!? Perhaps another day
Truth or lies? I don't care
I'm done listening anyway

Is that madness in your heart?
Do you worship the God of thunder?
Live or die? I don't care
It is time to kill and plunder

I do enjoy your ridiculous logic
Do you have that self righteous disease?
Saint or martyr? I don't care
Spending your life on your knees

Your insults are my kind words
I've been cut by your sharp tongue
Wasp or scorpion? I don't care
You're poisonous. I am stung

My Confession

Look right through you with my madman's gaze
You would ask for my confession?
Who are you to hear my sins?
It's not my faith that is in question

My soul will not be bought or broken
It's none of your business how I live
I do not accept your religion
My confession is mine to give

The new dawn creeps up on me
While I was looking at yesterday
I'll not confess my remorse or regret
The past is past. I'll no longer pay

By earth and water my soul's been purged
White lightning was my bane
My confession is not forthcoming
On my own, I will deal with my pain

On the edge of the abyss
Don't give into the monster's desire
You will never hear my confession
I'd rather be cleansed by fire

Patiently, the gallows are waiting
Step to the trap door. It's my time
There will be no last minute reprieve
I will not confess to any crime

You would give your strength to the weak?
Although this gift comes at a price
All it costs is my confession
No thanks. I'm grateful for the advice

You want me to tell you my secrets?
Sorry that's too much information
My confession shall remain private
Not to be told all over creation

I will not accept your judgement
That's your version of right and wrong
I won't confess to priest or pastor
I don't feel the need to belong

I'll confess that I'm happier now
Than I have been for a long long time
And I'll confess I have some demons
It remains an uphill climb

I'll confess I can't see the light
Unless the sun is in the sky
I'll confess I don't know what happens
To our consciousness after we die

I'll confess that I'm not perfect
And I'll confess that I've made mistakes
But I will not get into heaven
If a confession is what it takes

The End

On The Breeze

Oxygen and gasoline combust
I cannot see through the haze
The ignition takes my breath away
The morning mist is set ablaze

On my signal unleash hell
Remorse is a thing of the past
The flames of hell are relentless
My flickering shadow is all that's cast

The entire world is burning
It could surely mean certain death
The smoke is thick and acrid
One last final gasping breath

The curse of rage flows through my veins
Can you feel the heat of my desire
Light the fuse and run like hell
My soul has been purged by fire

Flying high on wings of fire
The brightness burns my eyes
Through the darkness I see the flames
The fire will burn and the smoke will rise

Out of the mountains comes the thunder
Lightning ignites the trees
Fire spreads all across the land
Sparks are carried on the breeze

Writhing Elegance

The moon slips in front of the sun
The fiery ring can blind you
The moon's shadow swallows the earth
In the daylight, it's shadow will find you

I have a bonfire in my backyard
I'm casting shadows on the trees
My shadow flickers and dances
I'm cleansed by the evening breeze

Casting shadows in the midday sun
My shadow has no fear in the light
Silence looms and darkness falls
My shadow can't be seen in the night

I do not have any peace of mind
My shadow follows me night and day
Ever present, but hidden in the dark
My stealthy shadow won't go away

My evil shadow, cast by hellfire
Writhing elegantly in the abyss
My shadow is all but erased
By the fire's delicate kiss

Nature's Beast

In the wilderness he roams
Killing machine in the moonlight
There's no malice in nature's beast
He kills to eat. Not for spite

In the wilderness he is king
Nature's beast rules all the land
If you run you're as good as dead
Turn and fight. Take a stand

In the dark his eyes are ablaze
Feel the power as the beast springs
The smell of death is all around him
The world still turns. The birds still sing

As if built out of thunder and steel
The beast's killer instinct is intense
Sharp eyes and fast as lightning
You can't hide. There's no defence

Nature's beast continues to hunt
Awesome power. Mighty jaws
Fight to the end for survival
To eat, he kills without pause

In a flash the beast upon you
Cringe in fear of the bloody rampage
The beast has no remorse or regret
Just primal fury and fierce rage

My Shadow Fades

There is no escape from my shadow
Even in the darkest night
I cannot hide from my shadow
It follows me at the speed of light

The shadow of the moon falls on me
It's dark but my shadow persists
It's relentless, it won't be stopped
My sanity has ceased to exist

The flaming horizon consumes me
My shadow is all that remains
My sinner's soul has been set free
My spirit runs free on the plains

My shadow has no pity
My shadow does not feel shame
It's like my shadow is made of stone
My shadow does not feel pain

The Sun's power is infinite
My shadow flourishes in the sunrise
Unable to break free of my shadow
It will not leave me upon my demise

Standing at the gates of heaven
My shadow fades, it's too bright
Blinding light is all around me
My shadow disappears in the light

A Way Of Life

Walk the earth inside my world
Obsessively headed west
Trying to catch the setting sun
Sunburn and blisters. I must be blessed

Creeping darkness inside my world
I cannot see. I am blind
The darkness is thick and complete
Slipping quietly through my mind

Storm of souls inside my world
My sanity's been torn asunder
I'm grieving the loss of my spirit
Deafened by crushing thunder

Angels sing inside my world
Beautiful like chirping birds
Melodic and hypocritical
Singing songs with empty words

White lightning inside my world
Delicate. Like swallowing fire
Slaughtering my innocence
White lightning. My only desire

Tattered and torn inside my world
I am nearly a broken man
I'm grieving the loss of my soul
Struck down by God's right hand

Burning fire inside my world
The flames are getting higher
I don't think God will save me
The situation is looking dire

Sleeping monster inside my world
Waiting to wake and attack
The monster is craving blood
He's right behind you. Don't look back

Sideways rain inside my world
My world is being torn apart
The storm is in a complete rage
The tornado is about to start

Whispering voices inside my world
It's better than when they shout
To the voices I am listening
It's time to let my demons out

A tooth for tooth inside my world
You have no remorse in the end
An eye for an eye might suffice
Vengeance is a way of life my friend

Tired and breathless inside my world
A look of desperation in my eyes
I am fleeing from my destiny
I have thrown away my disguise

The End

Relentless

My relentless pursuit of the storm
Has left me drowning in the rain
One last dance in the summer shower
The jungle rhythm eases my pain

My relentless pursuit of youth
Wasted years. I'm bitter and old
Always searching for the next thrill
My sinner's soul has been bought and sold

My relentless pursuit of sanity
Has not made me see the light
There is darkness all around me
I am stuck in perpetual night

My relentless pursuit of freedom
Has left me hopelessly confined
No hope for pardon or parole
The committal papers have been signed

My relentless pursuit of power
Has led to my annihilation
I am lost. Body and soul
Please witness my transformation

My relentless pursuit of peace
Has left me unfit to face the day
My apathy is unbecoming
In the asylum is where I'll stay

My relentless pursuit of vengeance
Has predictably taken it's toll
Hellbent on retribution
I'm grieving the loss of my soul

My relentless pursuit of truth
Has left me scratching my head
I'm a sinner. Guilty of life
Even the righteous will end up dead

My relentless pursuit of salvation
Sabotaged by a lack of belief
Attempted to pray with no results
The good Lord offered no relief

My relentless pursuit of pleasure
Has left me more weak than wise
None of it will matter in the end
The Reaper does not care for my cries

The End

Dragon's Kiss

A prophecy foretold in the whiskey
Kiss of the dragon is on your lips
Bunch of superstitious savages
It's nothing but a solar eclipse

Grief and pain all around me
Kiss of the dragon will save your soul
Living large in the asylum
I am a lunatic, I've lost control

You've spent your life in pursuit of truth
Kiss of the dragon will test your belief
Please mainline the medication
I want immediate relief

The blood moon is hanging low
Kiss of the dragon lights the sky
They say it's just a test of faith
Will you bother to ask why?
Feel the heat from its beating wings
Kiss of the dragon will bring death
Fire in the eyes of the beast
I can taste the dragon's rancid breath

The spirit of the beast is within me
Kiss of the dragon, remove all doubt
Black sky is without sympathy
The eternal fire has gone out

Touch The Sun

My mind is growing dim
There is no mercy in my eyes
My thoughts are getting hazy
Sanity is my favourite disguise

There is no time to waste
Zigzag lightning in the night
Thunder booms and the rain falls
See and hear this beautiful sight

Perfect strangers in the dark
Look for meaning in the sky
Searching for peace of mind
Waiting for my spirit to fly

The blood red sky is turning pink
A new day. The sun is on the rise
Shadows are dancing on the ground
The birds are flying in the skies

Four winds blow in the morning
The gentle rain is almost gone
Shadows creep in the morning mist
Stealthy as the silent dawn

I wish I could touch the sun
I can, when I close my eyes
I would lose myself in the fire
Perhaps I will upon my demise?

I Am Life

Embrace me. I am hope
I'm looking toward the sky
Riding carelessly on the wind
Soaring free. I've learned to fly

Enjoy me. I am pain
Grit your teeth. It just feels right
Pain and pleasure are synonymous
A dream? A nightmare? Not quite

Admire me. I am strong
You will not hear my confession
I will not follow the crowd
I will not ask for redemption

Judge me. I am sin
I am dirty I am flawed
Sinning's as natural as breathing
I'll not repent to man or God

Worship me. I am God
God of vengeance or God of mercy
I am real. Do not doubt me
The subject of great controversy

Adore me. I am thunder
I rumble and crash in the sky
Do not fear the thunderstorms
Wipe that tear from your eye

See me. I am justice
They say that I am blind
Tell that to the innocent man
Who's about to be confined

Listen to me. I am righteous
I will not whisper in your ear
I will preach loud and strong
Just to make sure you can hear

Forgive me. I am rude
I am short on etiquette
Unable to finish this verse
I'm no longer eloquent

Fear me. I am night
Creatures come out to play
I am the witching hour
For the gift of light many would pray

Touch me. I am bliss
I am soaring like a bird
Torn between sins of the flesh
And following God's good word

Smell me. I am fear
Do you fear life? Do you fear death?
Are you too scared to carry-on?
Will you savour your last breath?

Hear me I am ignorance
I have ridiculous logic
Living in oblivion
Stupidity is tragic

Commit me. I am insane
The voices are screaming
I'm raving in my padded cell
Catatonic. Am I dreaming?

Feed me. I am fire
I've a voracious appetite
Consuming everything in my path
My dancing flames will excite

Inhale me. I am smoke
I disappear in the breeze
Where there's smoke there's fire
Dancing merrily among the trees

Hold me. I am lightning
Zigzagging from the sky
Where I strike? You never know
I am lightning. I am sly

Heal me. I am disease
I'm the cause of great despair
I bring on desperation
Cause an atheist to say a prayer

Praise me. I am wicked
I'm not here to ease your pain
Like it or not we're born to die
Only dust and bones remain

Look at me. I am death
We will all return to dust
I wouldn't change a damn thing
Lived a life of sin and lust

In The Morning

Thunder and steel in the morning
Living is a work of art
Heaven or hell? Good or evil?
There is no conflict in my heart

Rain and wind in the morning
It soothes both mind and soul
A good day to brave the elements
The storm is not out of control

Living the dream in the morning
There's no sign left of the night
The new day's sun warms my bones
My sinner's soul takes flight

Power and glory in the morning
Is that a hole in the sky?
Can you picture the scene?
All of the birds take wing and fly

Distant thunder in the morning
It drowns out my fading cries
Looking for the meaning of life
I've no interest in your righteous lies

Fight for freedom in the morning
Peace of mind is elusive
Emotion and anger now control me
The situation is explosive

Sinners and saints in the morning
Can you spot the difference?
Who are you to judge anyway
You're showing your ignorance

An angel's kiss in the morning
There is madness all around
Am I going crazy?
My paranoia makes no sound

Tattered and torn in the morning
Surrounded by broken dreams
Dark thoughts swirl in my mind
Can you hear my silent screams?

Nothing to lose in the morning
Except my fragile sanity
I stand screaming at the clouds
Hear my righteous profanity

Doubts and fears in the morning
Are you feeling ill at ease?
Do you fear the future?
Death and destruction in the breeze

Smoke and wind in the morning
I don't think God is on my side
My final day has come and gone
On to eternity I ride

The End

Angels and Demons

Doubt and clarity haunt my thoughts
The constant doubt, I despise
Vision shrouded by uncertainty
Clarity. When I open my eyes

Fire and gasoline are devastating
The combination will excite
I can't take the anticipation
The world is about to ignite

Remorse and regret are useless
Only a fool lives in the past
Shame is a vicious animal
Beware. The Beast is coming fast

Lust and desire consume me
I think I'm about to explode
My urges are getting stronger
My restraint slowly erodes

Religion and belief are not the same
They're different ways to see the light
With religion you pay to pray
Belief will comfort you in the night

Anger and hate are an epidemic
Has all civility deceased?
I am not immune to the sickness
I dwell in the belly of the Beast

Heat and wind sweep across the land
Nuclear destruction on the plain
The dead are the fortunate ones
The cursed and the dying remain

Creeping and crawling through my nightmares
I'm not sure how much I can take
I'm hoping I don't die from fright
The problem is I'm still awake

Hard and fast are words to live by
Going through life at breakneck speed
Maybe I can outrun my illness
Pause for a moment, the Beast will feed

Voices and ruminations accost me
Living a visceral nightmare
Mental illness is a vicious Beast
Into it's eyes I continue to stare

Faith and dreams in the darkness
The concept overloads my brain
Lying awake under the stars
In the gentle predawn rain

Guilt and innocence are relative
Situational. Do you think you're pure?
You've avoided the hangman's noose
Perhaps the hangman is the cure

Sinners and saints question your faith
Poisonous shadows draw near
Ones fate is the same as the other
Your day of judgement is here

Life and death follow your heart
I have reached my limit of pain
We are all just walking corpses
Alive or dead. Don't complain

Hands and knees. I am crawling
Angry flames lick my skin
Smoke is filling the room
My eternity, about to begin

Angels and demons. Accept my fate
Both have come for my soul
Want to take me to Heaven or Hell
Eternal life. Pay the toll

The End

Don't Look Back

I don't remember my nightmares but
I have no dreams of dying
There is no escape from this hell
Shit. You aren't even trying

Are you looking for answers?
I'm afraid I have none to give
The beast is coming. It is pissed
Shit. You better run if you want to live

Beware. I am burning
I am the power of fire
Always hungry. Always eating
Shit. That is my desire

Do you stand for freedom?
Are you full of arrogance and greed?
Should I pray or unleash the thunder?
Shit. It's too late. Just proceed

Do you have the courage?
The courage to face your fears
I've been granted some kind of reprieve
Shit. This is better than I've been in years

Are you a victim of the beast?
The evidence is as plain as day
I don't look back or it'll catch you
Shit. You looked back anyway

I Am Fire

Finally Free

I am untamed fury
I am the smoke in your eyes
I am as hot as hell
I am fire. Reaching for the sky

I am insanity
I am here to devour
I am eating the world
I am fire. Feel the power

I am insatiable hunger
I am neither meek nor mild
I am the kiss of death
I am fire. Running wild

I am as ageless as time
I am without remorse
I am full of mischief
I am fire. I'll run my course

I am restless misery
I am the gift of pain
I am the darkness closing in
I am fire. Explode into flames

I am born to climb
I am reaching high
I am an inferno
I am fire. Refuse to die

I am a divine blessing
I am skin warming heat
I am a terrible curse
I am fire. No retreat

I am destruction
I am without control
I am your final breath
I am fire. I have no soul

I am a slow death
I am the elusive beast
I am hypnotically dancing
I am fire. I've been released

I am carried on the four winds
I am not afraid of dying
I am burning it down
I am fire. I'm terrifying

I am touching everything
I am killing your dreams
I am free as a bird
I am fire. I enjoy your screams

I am raw energy
I am jumping tree to tree
I am embers in the wind
I am fire. I'm finally free

A Crippling Display

A stunning display of apathy
Could you possibly care less?
Smile. A new day is dawning
I'm indifferent too. I must confess

An awesome display of deception
Your morals are lost in the sun
Empty promises surround you
Your dishonesty is just begun

A shoddy display of perfection
You have fucked it up again
Your incompetence will blossom
It's not a matter of if. It's when

A vulgar display of lust
How can I stoke the fire?
There is passion on the wind
Feed my appetite. My only desire

A profound display of depression
Are you able to face the day?
The seeds of despair have been sown
Your entire world is black and grey

A disappointing display of the truth
You make the truth sound like lies
I sense no remorse in you
There are no tears in your cold eyes

A gross display of power
Are you flaunting your might?
Do you strike like lightning?
Then fade back into the night

A shackled display of freedom
If you are free, why don't you sing
Talk of riot and rebellion
I'll no longer kneel before the king

A crippling display of force
Man's decimation is in the breeze
War and death are in the air
Nuclear winter. The world will freeze

A dazzling display of destruction
Chaos and pain throughout the land
Can you rise above the ruin?
Start over. Right back where we began

The End

No Longer Missed

No longer guilty
No longer to blame
No longer innocent
No longer feel shame

No longer shining
No longer bright
No longer justified
No longer right

No longer a fool
No longer a clown
No longer suicidal
No longer down

No longer chaotic
No longer wild
No longer innocent
No longer a child

No longer angry
No longer pissed
No longer matter
No longer missed

No longer chained
No longer bound
No longer lost
No longer found

No longer asleep
No longer dreaming
No longer in pain
No longer screaming

No longer a lunatic
No longer crazy
No longer confused
No longer hazy

No longer incarcerated
No longer in a cage
No longer biding my time
No longer in a rage

No longer religious
No longer praying
No longer ignorant
No longer obeying

No longer in shadows
No longer in the night
No longer misguided
No longer chasing the light

No longer dishonest
No longer lying
No longer breathing
No longer dying

The End

Wrath of the Gods

There is darkness inside my world
There is desperation in my eyes
My world is crumbling around me
The God of Despair is on the rise

Fight for freedom under the stars
I'm grieving the loss of my soul
Screaming savagery from on high
The God of Thunder has lost control

Are you here to save my soul?
If so. Could you please do it fast
I am fighting for my life
The God of Disease. I'm not going to last

The nightmare begins in earnest
Single minded in his desire
Do you think you can save your soul
The God of the Damned spewing Hell fire

I don't care if you believe or not
He is real you can't deny
Slash like lightning. Crash like thunder
The God of Pain comes down from the sky

Chaotic perfection in action
Bomb and bullet. Rip skin. Shatter bone
Reducing men to hair and meat
The God of War. His ravens have flown

Yesterday's promises have been broken

With no emotions except hate
Retribution is on his mind
The God of Vengeance. Come meet your fate

Imprisoned for eternity
Freedom is only a dream
Naked and breathless in my world
The God of lust is obscene

There is no sign of danger
The fire is burning bright
Without warning he approaches
The God of Death stalks the nightl

Caught in the teeth of the storm
Devastation is in the air
Breathing lightning and uprooting trees
The God of destruction. Say a prayer

Power and glory in the west
The eternal sun sinks into the earth
Again tomorrow, it will rise
The God of Light. Witness his rebirth

The End

Raven's Roost

Dead silence in the shadow of the moon
The Indifferent raven with vacant eyes
I am damned in the darkness
Out of the gloom the raven flies

Are you imprisoned for eternity?
The unbound raven is flying
A flash of lightning in your soul
The flash of lightning's electrifying

Relentlessly eating the world
The innocent raven is blameless
Dead or alive. It's not picky
A carrion bird. It is shameless

Fire in it's brain and ice in it's heart
The wise Raven has dead black eyes
Are you predator or prey?
Is this the day of your demise?

The hillside is alive with the dead
The scavenging ravens are squawking
Fierce warrior on the battlefield
In the night the Reaper's stalking

Longing and lust are in the breeze
The greedy raven can't hide it's desire
Cloaked in mystery and deceit
Crafty raven roosting on barbwire

The solar eclipse is perfect
The hungry raven begins to eat
A swift death is not my fate
I am doomed. I'm made of meat

My fate remains hidden
The blind raven has lost its sight
Aimlessly flying into oblivion
It's eyes burnt by the brilliant light

Surveying the battlefield
The patient raven awaits
The hand of doom destroys
Struck down by the hand of fate

Waiting patiently at Heaven's Gate
The wily raven is not sad
Scavenging upon the earth
It's the best time he ever had

The raven wants to consume me
The solemn raven. Worlds collide
Thunderous hooves across the sky
Horsemen of the apocalypse ride

My fragile bones will become dust
The heartless raven will set me free
I am not a righteous soul
Where will I spend eternity?

The End

I Must Be Blessed

Ride the wind to the promised land
The magnificent view will amaze
Like an eagle. I am soaring
My body disappears in the haze

Ride the wind to paradise
Do you know the secret of flight?
Is euphoria what you seek?
Flying high through the night

Ride the wind to Valhalla
I will not relinquish my sword
Been blessed by the God of War
My faith has been restored

Ride the wind to eternity
We will all feel death's sweet kiss
Deeds of valour go unnoticed
They say ignorance is bliss

Ride the wind to the eye of the storm
Is it just merciful fate
An oasis of serenity
In a world of violence and hate

Ride the wind to the sunset
I continue to look to the west
I am flying in the sunshine
Truly. I must be blessed

In The Valley

Fire and flames all around me
Battle cry in the Valley of Kings
Fighting beneath the blazing sun
Steel on steel. Hear the savage ring

Maces smash and axes cleave
Blood and gore in the Valley of Kings
Prepare for death's black embrace
Flyaway on the Devil's wing

Are you still courageous and brave?
Raise your voice in the Valley of Kings
A legend is born on the battlefield
The killing blade continues to swing

Battle fever. I feel no pain
Fallen hero in the Valley of Kings
Deeds of valour will be forgotten
Hero. Killed by the arrow's sweet sting

Will the ancient one set me free?
Starving now, in the Valley of Kings
Flying away on the wings of a dream
Drifting away as the angels sing

Staring into the eye of the sun
No grave in the Valley of Kings
Ruler of the kingdom of sand
Listen. You can hear the vultures sing

Sly Sunlight

The sunlight is just below the horizon
The new dawn is glowing bright
Ever present. Ever shining
I will welcome back the dark of night

The sunlight is Inevitable
Time stands still as the sun ascends
Apprehension is in the air
I wish the night would never end

The sunlight chases away the shadows
The ominous dawn makes not a sound
Look and listen as the sun rises
The ravens are singing all around

The sunlight smoulders in the east
The moon is still in the sky
Count the seconds. Can you feel it?
Beware the sunlight is sly

The sunlight seeps in my sealed window
Stealthily creeping across the floor
Slowly slipping across the room
Across the carpet and up the door

The sunlight touches everything
Gently caressing my existence
Nothing is left unmolested
It shows relentless insistence

The sunlight touches me. I'm sill cold
Years of sinning have take their toll
I'm freezing to death in the light of day
It warms my skin but not my soul

The sunlight is throwing shadows
There are gravestones in my eyes
I enjoy the darkness in my heart
It's the sunshine I've come to despise

The sunlight is predictable
I feel dread but no danger
It enters the room quietly
Like an unwelcome stranger

The sunlight is torture
When will this Hell be ending
Rising until it can't anymore
Then slowly descending

The sunlight hurts my eyes
The light is finally receding
But the damage has been done
My fragile soul is bleeding

The sunlight has been exposed
But the night fills me with wonder
Will you join my delusion?
Enjoy the sound of rolling thunder

The sunlight is Hell on earth
Recoiling from it's unwanted touch
I don't crave it's superficial heat
That's asking a little too much

The sunlight is constantly creeping
It's playing tricks with my mind
Patiently feeling everything
The sunlight seeks to strike me blind

The sunlight steals my dreams
Can't breathe in the morning mist
Staring down the barrel of a new day
By my delusions I've been kissed

The sunlight burns my eyes
Another tomorrow has arrived
Standing on the edge of forever
Will this day be survived?

The sunlight is relentless
There is fear in my bright blue eyes
I am full of dread and despair
Ever since the sun began to rise

The sunlight has poisoned my mind
Am I the last person on earth?
I'm a different man in the sunshine
Did you witness my rebirth?

The sunlight seems out to get me
My paranoia. My disgrace
I'm no longer scared of the night
I don't fear it's dark embrace

The sunlight peeks over the horizon
I feel no joy. I feel only despair
Waiting for the night to return
Waiting for the darkness to fill the air

The sunlight makes me anxious
With the sunshine comes the fear
Do you think you're safe in the daytime?
Think again. The beast is near

The End

Are You A Messiah

Are you a serene Messiah
The sun's high in the afternoon sky
The wind blows gently at the river
Look up. Stare your lord in the eye

Are you a wiser messiah?
Your morbid beliefs baffle me
I will not crawl at your feet
Is your faith based in reality

Are you a warrior Messiah
A pleased expression on your face
The God of War has smiled on you
You will not die in disgrace

Are you a bipolar Messiah
You're completely out of control
You've been released upon the world
Crippling depression in your soul

Are you the straitjacket Messiah?
Tied up wearing a lunatic's grin
It's time to ride the lightning
I'll hook you up and we'll begin

Are you a false Messiah?
Do you practice what you preach?
Are you getting off on violence?
Do you learn from the lessons you teach?

Are you a deceptive messiah
Are you crazy? Why would you lie?
All I hear is you flapping your lips
I see through your bullshit. Nice try

Are you a burning Messiah
Lit by your fury. The world ignites
First smoldering. Then raging
Your eyes are burning. You've lost your sight

Are you a grim Messiah?
No shadows for there is no light
I am at home in the darkness
I am a creature of the night

Are you a feral Messiah?
Do you have to kill to eat?
Stalking your prey in the darkness
Ravenous. In search of fresh meat

Are you a dark Messiah?
Is your passion fading away?
Are you reduced to ashes?
By the sun of the new day?

Are you a wicked Messiah?
Lust and power are in your eyes
Are you the Devil's right hand man?
Are you exuding wrath and despise?

Are you a vengeful Messiah
It's pitch black in your padded cell
They will eventually release you
When they do you'll unleash hell

Are you dying Messiah?
Are you living for today?
Are you running out of time?
Is your face an ashen grey?

Are you a deceased Messiah
Sailing away into the unknown
Your final words are your epitaph
Which is carved upon your tombstone

The End

The Hurricane

Search the sky for the hurricane
It's full of beautiful things
The sun is high. The birds are flying
Wait to see what tomorrow brings

Scream and shout at the hurricane
My sanity is lost in the breeze
The wind is wet and fierce
Blowing down houses. Uprooting trees

Flying high through the hurricane
Is this a hallucination
Immense. The storm is a monster
It could flood the entire nation

Tattered and torn in the hurricane
The icy wind is cold
I'm questioning my immortality
I will not be growing old

Angel of death in the hurricane
Are you ready to die
No escaping the inevitable
Hang on. You will to learn to fly

A new dawn after the hurricane
I don't know if I should laugh or cry
The storm is gone just like a dream
The impassive dawn has no reply

Time To Rise

Looking back
Days gone by
Full of regret
Sit and cry

The face of evil.
That's not me
My heart is pure
Just let me be

Eternity beckons
Ageless as time
Impending death
No one's fault but mine

Flawed creature
Nobody's perfect
Doing my best
No respect

Blaze of glory
Final breath
Battle cry
Senseless death

Life and death
Just states of mind
The night's truth
Morally blind

Hand of doom
My true shadow
Alive or dead
I don't know

The ground trembles.
You approach
Man or beast
Creatures encroach

Seeds of doubt
Sleepless night
Religion
A reason to fight

Taste the medicine
Agony remains
Running out of life
No more earthly pains

Fallen Angel
Concedes his wings
Lucifer descends
Hell's choir sings

Winds of salvation
Somebody cries
Resurrection
Time to rise

The End

Chaos Is Perfection

Truth is situational
Your perspective. Your lies
Backed up by empty promises
Fear and loathing in disguise

Justice is irrelevant
I pulled the trigger in my mind
I've been accused and convicted
Though I have committed no crime

Freedom is unattainable
My fight for liberty has gone awry
I'm like a bird in a gilded cage
No longer free. I cannot fly

Mania is euphoric
Feel invincible. Feel so strange
The mania has me in it's clutches
I am perfect. Why should I change

Rage is contagious
Quiet. You'll wake the Beast
Like a flame it spreads
Once contained. Now released

Chaos is perfection
The rebellion is in full swing
Let anarchy rule the day
Fly away on the Devil's wing

Apocalypse is destruction
Lightning. There's fire in the sky
The storm is in a frenzy
Ready or not it's time to die

Existence is fleeting
The sun reveals it's golden light
Could it be that we're immortal?
Hard to believe in the dark of night

Religion is baffling
The world has gone insane
Anarchy. The perfect distraction
The church is engulfed in flame

Salvation is elusive
The seconds keep ticking away
Find your way out of the darkness
Out of the night. Into the light of day

Doom is impending
Army of steel is still fighting
The screams of chaos break my mind
No more screams. The noose is tightening

The End

Shh

Shh. Please. I must close my eyes
The light is driving me insane
Insanity is just a state of mind
Love the madness. Enjoy the pain

Shh. Please. Hit me with the lightning
Frightened. The darkness is all around
The very next flash could blind me
All that's left is that sizzling sound

Shh. Please. Love it to death
The bad old days are gone for good
I feel battered and violated
Abused but as tough as wood

Shh. Please. Take the bullet
Brace yourself. Can you feel the thunder?
You would sacrifice yourself for me?
I am perplexed and full of wonder

Shh. Please. Mourn my final breath
The rumours of my death are true
I heard the raven call my name
Surely it was meant for you

Shh. Please. Let my spirit soar
I feel at peace. It's mystifying
The view takes my breath away
I've been set free. I am flying

Shh. Please. Save my soul
My body is no longer strong
Anticipating my demise
I've been waiting for so damn long

Shh. Please. I'm slightly insane
Mental illness is not a sin
A long day of acting normal
Feeling strange in my own skin

Shh. Please. Dare to dream
Don't just sit there and pout
The whole world is not a nightmare
Find a way to let my demons out

Shh. Please leave me alone
I have no interest in your blessing
I'm by no means an evil man
But is that the Beast I'm caressing?

Shh. Please. Just tell the truth
I cannot take anymore lies
All your bullshit and half truths
It's you I've come to despise

Shh. Please. Let me sleep
I must spend some time relaxing
It's not easy to rise from the dead
My resurrection was very taxing

Shh. Please. Stop this test of faith
The past. I no longer want to die
My faith is stagnant. My flesh is weak
I don't know if I should laugh or cry

The End

Cries of War

Cries of war fill the air
My heart pounds on the battlefield
Gripped in my strong right hand
My gleaming sword I will wield

Charging into the great unknown
Spilling blood on the battlefield
I have long waited for this day
No quarter. I will never yield

Live for honor, death and glory
Final stand on the battlefield
The enemy flees before me
My rage will not be concealed

Victory or death. Time will tell
Darkness descends on the battlefield
The moon fills the misty sky
My fate has been sealed

Steel cleaves muscle and bone
I am killed on the battlefield
Can you hear the ravens cry
My mortality has been revealed

It was a glorious death
My spirit departs battlefield
The ravens and crows will be fed
Before God or king I did not kneel

The Charming Serpent

The charming serpent is beautiful
He has exquisite eyes
There is hope and faith in them
He'd make you believe all his lies

The charming serpent is a legend
Do you believe the earth is round
Round or flat he doesn't care
He'll burn the world to the ground

The charming serpent is whispering
He's full of lies and deceit
He has a heinous spirit
Silver tongued. His words are sweet

The charming serpent is venomous
It's poison is subtle but strong
It's deadly but it's intoxicating
It feels so good it must be wrong

The charming serpent is wily
Shrewd. He knows time is on his side
Underneath the fiery moon
He feels his actions are justified

The charming serpent is brazen
Bold and shameless in his actions
The end justifies the means
Will you get some satisfaction?

The charming serpent is fierce
He will fight you to the death
Vigourous and powerful
He will inhale your last breath

The charming serpent is immense
You may tremble. Marvel at his girth
Full of a sly determination
He spreads his curse across the earth

The charming serpent is ancient
As old as the blazing sun?
Is it a question of good versus evil
Has the apocalypse begun?

The charming serpent is cunning
His existence he'll deny
The charming serpent shows no mercy
Life is short and then you die

The charming serpent is not dead
Though he would have you grieve
He is not innocent or benign
As he'd like you to believe

The charming serpent is lethal
But rather than bite you. He'll lie
The serpent could kill you in an instant
But he wants you to suffer, not die

The End

Smiles Or Tears

Do you think you can save the world
Fire on the earth and in the sky
The howling wind causes a frenzy
Sparks and embers fly

It's time to fight for your life
Search for the truth in the smoke
What have I got to lose?
I feel so alive as I cough and choke

Are you able to save this world
The inferno is out of control
Make no mistake. This won't be survived
God have mercy on my sinner's soul

The destroyer is on a rampage
Like a madman in a house of mirrors
There is shattered glass all around
What do you expect? Smiles or tears?

Breathing. I make not a sound
Silent as the breaking dawn
Can you see the sun in the sky
In the breeze. My remorse is all gone

My back is against the wall
I'm sick. Can you see it in my eyes
The thunder roars in my ears
The world burns and my spirits rise

Saint Vincent

Saint Vincent is a fortunate sinner
I escaped the noose's sweet embrace
I'll remain honourable to the end
I'll not spend eternity in disgrace

Saint Vincent is a changed sinner
I survived years of insanity
They tried to cure me with religion
I'll not embrace Christianity

Saint Vincent is a charming sinner
I am not an arrogant Saviour
I will not beg forgiveness
For all my years of bad behaviour

Saint Vincent is lucky sinner
The Devil's footsteps are retreating
Saint Vincent is a lucky sinner
These six words bear repeating

Saint Vincent is a fierce sinner
I have avoided the slaughter
Feeling stronger than ever before
Spent all those years treading water

Saint Vincent is a hopeful sinner
I made it out more alive than dead
I was an unwilling victim
Better things are just ahead

Saint Vincent is a mortal sinner
There is no way to cheat death
At one time I would've welcomed it
Now I savour every breath

Odin's Birds

The crafty raven has no emotions
With feathers as black as coal
And an appetite for death
The raven. Can't save my soul

Thunder rolls and lightning crashes
They say there's no sadness in the light
Not waiting for good weather
The raven. Flies through the stormy night

The trees creak. The leaves rustle
The wind is whispering in my ear
The harbinger of death croaks
The raven. The messenger of fear

I wear bravery like a mask
There's no more need for my disguise
There'll be no survivors except
The raven. With black beady eyes

Welcome the sunshine from above
My horror I cannot conceal
I know I'm about to be eaten
The raven. It's beak as sharp as steel

In the heat of the battle
I have paid the ultimate price
It will get my body but not my soul
The raven. Say goodbye to Paradise

I've been walking in the shadows
I appear to be one of the slain
To be consumed by the scavengers
The raven. Wild blood in it's veins

Sitting in the morning sun
I no longer have the strength to fight
Tomorrow is just a dream
The raven. Hunting by sight

Battling the sun in the wasteland
Are you getting ready to die?
Look in the eyes of your salvation
The raven. Circling the sky

In the heat of battle
Death is just another word
Thought and memory bring tidings
The raven. Odin's birds

Scavenging the land
Thousands and thousands have died
Returning the dead to the soil
The raven. Are you terrified?

Feeling depressed as I realize
This life will not be survived
With sharp claws and it's savage beak
The raven. Eat you dead or alive

The End

Fallen Angel

Clenching my teeth and holding my breath
I plummet like a stone from the sky
Thrown from Heaven by a vengeful God
I swear to God, I thought I could fly

Free falling through nothingness
The air offers little resistance
I am no longer righteous
I hear God laughing in the distance

Time seems to standstill
Look and listen. Are you terrified
Falling at the speed of fear
Can't enjoy it. I'm petrified

No time to think or react
Memories rising in my mind
I will receive no second chance
My death warrant has been signed

I really don't like my choices
Earth or hell. Where will I land
Either crash down on the earth
Or caught in the Devil's right hand

I am screaming through the clouds
Surrounded by a sea of white
Frozen seconds. Time stands still
Desperately seeking the light

No longer mocking religion
I pray. Though God himself cast me out
Below the clouds now. I see the ground
It's time for me to scream and shout

The judgement bell is tolling
I can hear it as plain as day
An angel stripped of its wings
For my pride I must pay

I have run out of options
I seek the truth. But it hides
This is it. The end of the line
In my heart is where fear resides

The earth is the rushing towards me
There is no way to slow down
Time to brace for impact
I'll become one with the ground

This fallen angel is no longer pure
Nor am I a creature of evil
Cast out by a vengeful God
Should I pray for my soul's retrieval?

My life only has seconds left
The ground is before my eyes
A long fall with a sudden stop
No one cares for my demise

The End

Nothing Personal

Darkness quickly descends
Wolves are howling in the distance
Beware of the creatures of the night
Flesh and bone offer little resistance

Smell of death pervades the world
The mighty wolf cannot be subdued
I cannot escape the creature
To him I am nothing but food

The wolf is hunger. The wolf lust
Craving to dine on humanity
No where to run. Living is madness
You will forfeit your sanity

Caress the snarling beast
It's claws dig deep into my flesh
About to be devoured by the wolf
Better eat while the meat's still fresh

The wolf is built to ravage
To cross it's path is certain death
It's nothing personal
It will steal your last breath

There is no joy in his actions
It's just instinct not the thrill of the kill
He's just trying to survive
Eat till he gets his fill

Deadly Beaks

Raven God on his ebony throne
The dark conceals creatures of the night
Stone cold killers with vacant eyes
Unkindness of ravens hunting by sight

Face to face with Mother Nature
Touch the sky with my right hand
The angel of death approaches
Wake of buzzards circle the wasteland

Black skies on the horizon
All of my hope has come and gone
There is no mercy in their eyes
Murder of crows flies in at dawn

Mother nature is victorious
I'll fly away on the devil's wing
The birds are hungry and ready to eat
Kettle of vultures begins to sing

Their deadly beaks are sharply honed
Their feathers glisten in the light
Their eyes are as black as their soul
Convocation of eagles takes flight

Starless darkness embraces me
My crumbling faith will endure
Man is a plague on the earth
Conspiracy of ravens is the cure

The Darkness

Smiling serpent in the darkness
Believing that he can't be seen
Crosses his heart and says his prayers
Sinner? Saint? Something in between?

My mind's in turmoil in the darkness
Voices and paranoia take their toll
Looking for any kind of escape
Whiskey and carrot cake saved my soul

Man of God in the darkness
I have no idea what you're saying
Righteous mumbling and grand gestures
To the good Lord are you praying?

Fight for your life the darkness
This battle will be to the death
I am the destroyer
Come. Inhale my rancid breath

Sweet vengeance in the darkness
My true intentions have been revealed
Twisting and turning in the wind
My hatred is no longer concealed

No retreat in the darkness
Stand tall. Never back down
My attack shall be like thunder
Zigzag lightning all around

I'll cut you down in the darkness
There will be no more light
To beg for mercy is futile
See my desire. Fear my appetite

Beg forgiveness in the darkness
That's some pretty odd behaviour
Would you repent for a million sins
Don't look at me. I'm not your saviour

Craving meat in the darkness
I'm a savage with vacant eyes
Run for your life if you wish
My hunger will tell you no lies

Eyes of fire in the darkness
Let me introduce you to the beast
If you'd like I'll say Grace
In preparation for the coming feast

Impending doom in the darkness
I really don't like my chances
My back is up against the wall
Hold my breath as the creature advances

A legend is born in the darkness
Warrior king spilling blood
All flee before his wrath
Or die screaming in the mud

The End

Haunted

Beasts and creatures haunt me
Monsters are crawling in the night
In the darkness they lie in wait
I fear their claws and their appetite

Fire and flames haunt me
The smoke eclipses the sun
Looks like night in the afternoon
Mother Nature has been undone

Voices and lunacy haunt me
I've reevaluated my dreams
Now I wish for sanity but
I'm in the asylum with my screams

Dread and doom haunt me
Can you hear the raven scream
Listen closely. You may hear it
The soft whisper of the death machine

Thunder and lightning haunt me
Fear has gripped me and won't let go
The vicious thunder is raging
The north wind begins to blow

Shadows and darkness haunt me
Lightning touches earth and tree
In the treetops we have ignition
The animal has been set free

Blindness and frustration haunt me
There's a searing pain in my eyes
Mother Nature has cheated me
I cannot see my final sunrise

Crazy delusions haunt me
The Devil's choir softly sings
I'll rise up and be liberated
Flying free on a Raven's wings

Despair and apathy haunt me
I'm caught in a waking nightmare
Would you takeaway tomorrow?
Do you think anyone would care?

Fright and panic haunt me
Brokenhearted and alone
My pleas for mercy fall on deaf ears
My cries wasted on your heart of stone

Dreams and nightmares haunt me
Life is something to endure
Voices plague my waking hours
It's nothing a bullet wouldn't cure

Death and dying haunt me
The truth hits me like lightning
There's a time to live and time to die
Will death be enlightening?

The End

Plummeting

Cold and dark in the stratosphere
Fallen angel plummets from the sky
Fallen angel has lost his wings
He can no longer fly

Are you a creature of the night?
Fallen angel the darkness will hide you
Fallen angel screaming at shadows
Your no longer holy? Is it true?

Not immune to superstition
Fallen angel prays to the Lord
Fallen angel will repent
He fears God's righteous sword

The Lord's voice echoing in his head
Fallen angel covers his ears
Fallen angel is going insane
Must confront his psychotic fears

The horizon crumbles in the distance
Fallen angel covers his eyes
Fallen angel tries to hide from God
Righteousness. His favourite disguise

Is that fire and brimstone I smell?
Fallen angel your eyes are burning
Fallen angel it's plain as day
You're in the wind twisting and turning

Entranced

Darkness. Clouds rolling in
Hope. Been dry so long
Growl. Thunder in the distance
Rhythmic. The rain is singing it's song

Crash. Of the thunderbolt
Silence. Makes no sound
Rain. Unrelenting
Mud. Covers the ground

Lightning. Descends
Zigzag. Stick of fire
Flash. Expose the shadows
Storm. Pure desire

Downpour. Torrential
Pelted. Icy rain
Shiver. Freezing cold
Numb. Feel no pain

Rage. Life is a beast
Madman. Screaming at the sky
Living. Borrowed time
Blessed. I will never die

Thunder. Massive roar
Shouting. To be heard
Silence. In the aftermath
Choke. On God's good word

Fear. Starting to shake
Courage. Hold on tight
Lightning. Rips the sky
Blinded. By it's light

Eyes. Struck blind
Ears. Can no longer hear
Mind. Unable to think
Scared. Living in fear

Lightning. Strikes the treetops
Instantly. It ignites
Fledgling. Fire appears
Growing. It's fierce appetite

Flames. Starting to dance
Burn. Righteous power
Inhale. Soot and smoke
Fading. My final hour

Lightning. At my feet
Massive. Crash of thunder
Rain. Continues to fall
Crash. World torn asunder

Questions. Very few answers
Destiny. Also called fate
Death. Non-negotiable
Patience. Heaven can wait

Faith. It's slipping away
Belief. Never was that strong
Futile. We're living to die
Pious. Sing me a righteous song

Sparks. Are dancing
Crackling. The forest is burning
Flames. Lick the sky
Relentless. The world's still turning

Smoke. Black and thick
Dread. Alive and well
Whispering. Tales of doom
Inferno. Welcome to Hell

Chilling. Fear in my bones
Moon. Obscured by smoke
Fear. All consuming
Can't breathe. Cough and choke

Staring. I'm mesmerized
Entranced. By the fire
Reality. The spell is broken
Escape. My only desire

Raining. Sparks and embers
Fire. All around me
Pain. It is real
No choice. I've got to flee

Running. As fast as I can
Useless. Too little too late
Arrived. Point of no return
Deadly. The Hand of Fate

Looking. Up into the sky
Praying. To the God of Thunder
Silence. There's no reply
No response. No wonder

Solitude. I'm all alone
Breathless. Silent screams
Heat. Sears and burns
Stolen. My hopes and dreams

Escape. Just a fantasy
Falling. Rain of fire
Anger. In my heart and mind
LIve. My only desire

Lunatic. Running in circles
Insane. With misery and pain
Ringed. By smoke and flames
No doubt. I am to blame

Death. Raining down
Coughing. The smoke is winning
No answer. From the God of Thunder
I'm damned. From years of sinning

Gripped. By sorrow and sadness
Pissed off. Also in a rage
Impotent. Nobody cares
Remain calm. No time to rampage

Choking. Smoke in my lungs
Suffocation. Better than burning
Time stops. I'll get no older
Rumination. My mind's still churning

Fire. I'm surrounded
Smoke. Takes my breath away
Fire. Burns my hair and skin
Smoke. I'll not see a new day

Fire. Scorching me head to toe
Fire. I wish I was numb
Smoke. I'm passing out
Smoke. It's time to succumb

Unconscious. No longer aware
Listen. Do you hear the choir
Inhale. Nothing but smoke
Body and soul. Consumed by fire

Recycled. Circle of life
Fertilize. Mother Earth
Body. Devoured by the blaze
Witness. My soul's rebirth

The End

www.ingramcontent.com/pod-product-compliance
Lightning Source LLC
Chambersburg PA
CBHW021122080526
44587CB00010B/604